Say So

CLEVELAND STATE UNIVERSITY POETRY CENTER

NEW POETRY
Michael Dumanis, Series Editor

For a complete listing of titles please visit
www.csuohio.edu/poetrycenter

Washington College, 2011

Say So

For Jenna-

poems

Dora Malech

Cleveland State University Poetry Center
Cleveland, Ohio

ISBN 978-1-880834-92-3

First edition

5 4 3 2 1

This book is published by
Cleveland State University Poetry Center,
2121 Euclid Avenue, Cleveland, Ohio 44115-2214.
www.csuohio.edu/poetrycenter and is distributed by
SPD /Small Press Distribution, Inc. www.spdbooks.org

Cover image: *Heart Shadow,* by Laurel Nakadate.
Back cover image: *untitled (say so),* by Laurel Nakadate.
Copyright Laurel Nakadate, Courtesy Leslie Tonkonow
Artworks+Projects, NY

Say So was designed and typeset by Amy Freels in Optima,
with Trebuchet display.

LIBRARY OF CONGRESS CATALOGING-IN-PUBLICATION DATA
Malech, Dora.
Say so : poems / Dora Malech. — 1st ed.
     p. cm. — (New poetry)
ISBN 978-1-880834-92-3 (alk. paper)
I. Title. II. Series.
PS3613.A43523s29 2010
811'.6—DC22
                                        2010023934

Acknowledgments

Thanks to the editors of the following journals that first published these poems:

American Letters & Commentary: "Some Speech"
                                  "Sound Bites"
Anti-:   "Ante"
                                  "Our Fair Sentence"
                                  "Remains"
Barn Owl Review: "The Station"
Barrow Street: "Joyride"
The Canary: "Pocket Money"
                                  "Smart Money"
Chelsea: "Cold Weather"
                                  "God Bless Our Mess"
                                  "Small Ending"
                                  "Some Figures"
Columbia Poetry Review: "My First Creation Myth"
                                  "Oh Grow Up"
                                  "Oh My Obit"
                                  "The End"
Denver Quarterly: "Respects"
                                  "Thread the Needle"
Forklift, Ohio: "Flight, Fight Or"
Gargoyle: "Goodbye, I Love You"
                                  "Open Letter"
Indiana Review: "Physical Education"
Ink Node: "Copy That"
                                  "Lying Down with Dogs"
                                  "Relatively Long Arms"
La Petite Zine: "Where Babies Come From"
LIT: "Dancing with Strangers"

Mangrove:	"Trick or Treat"
New Orleans Review:	"A Light Touch"
	"The Little Hours"
No Tell Motel:	"Fiddler's Money"
	"Forever Hold Your Peace, Speak Now Or"
	"Note to So Sorry for Self"
	"Go, Touch And"
	"Heaven"
	"Hush Money"
	"Inventing the Body"
	"Pop Quiz"
	"Score"
	"Spectrum"
Painted Bride Quarterly:	"Love Poem"
Post Road:	"Face for Radio"
	"Quick Study"
Redivider:	"Consolation Prize"
	"I'm Rubber, You're Glue"
Sawbuck:	"Can't Get There from Here"
	"Director's Cut"
	"Getting Cold, Eh?"
	"Speech! Speech!"
Sonora Review:	"A man"
Sport:	"Flora and Fauna"
	"My Kingdom for the Pretty Picture"
	"Self-Portrait with Family Tree"
Thermos online:	"Break, Make Or"
	"Them's Fighting Words"
Tight:	"Canzone: How To"
Yale Review:	"The Kisser"

Thanks to the editors of Duets Books for publishing some of these poems in the chapbook *Pocket Money*.

for Jim

Contents

Say So

Some Figures

On any given morning even in this smallest of towns
one glove stranded on the convenience store linoleum
is rendering its partner's careless carcass elsewhere obsolete.

And on the given morning's given night before I am betting
low and losing at a table bearing scars. Innumerable crows pock
the trees and then give themselves up to the sky scattering

at the shots of a military funeral and this is happening
and this is happening again. The facts, my friend:
one in three primary colors is blue and the meters dream

of quarters seven times an hour even in the empty lot
at night and an ache that begins in a weak knee spreads word
of its aching so that each bone cries out in its sleep and when I tell

you I sat down to write a poem about how much I love you you will
not believe me and do on any given day not believe me even when
I touch your any given face and tell you and then try again.

Smart Money

Protagonist's protégé spit-shines the stop signs,
sits in her slip at the escritoire,
pens invitations, folds each kitten
a cootie-catcher. Sits on Daddy's
spectacles and begs a tall tale.
Pads bra with shredded resumes.
Pads bra with rifle wadding. Hey—
hook and ladder—this fire's a keeper.
A regular match—*your Hancock, my thorax*.
Inked up her navel, stole the X
clear out the alphabet and into
fable scrawled on butcher paper,
up for air to glimpse apocalypse
writ large in lipstick on the bathroom mirror.

Love Poem

If by *truth* you mean *hand* then yes
I hold to be self-evident and hold you in the highest—
K.O. to my O.T. and bait to my switch, I crown
you one-trick pony to my one-horse town,
dub you my one-stop shopping, my space heater,
juke joint, tourist trap, my peep show, my meter reader,
you best batteries-not-included baring all or
nothing. Let me begin by saying *if he hollers,*
end with *goes the weasel.* In between,
cream filling. *Get over it,* meaning, *the moon.*
Tell me you'll dismember this night forever,
you my punch-drunking bag, tar to my feather.
More than the sum of our private parts, we are some
peekaboo, some peak and valley, some
bright equation (if *and* then *but*, if *er* then *uh*).
My fruit bat, my gewgaw. You had me at *no duh.*

Inventing the Body

The lungs were my idea.
Shins, his.
Breasts, mine, though he agreed.

He tried to name his favorite organ
Mr. Winky, but titles were forbidden from the start.

Laughter was a vital sign,
amended to a ticking in the chest.

We called the heart the heart
because we could not say its real name,
even to each other, even in the dark.

Oh Grow Up

First thing's first aid and off-track
abetting, next best bloodshot, blood-work,
smarmy reprimand commanding indoor voices,
some chomping at the little bit small choice
of soup or nut or thrum or hustle. Honey, clinch
or canyon? Working girls include wicked witch
of the Western omelet, she of the one night best for last
stand. Last gal standing. Fat lip and a canker, fat
chance of better bodywork or better business
as usual smuggled tub of butter pecan. Yes
yes, hit you, and yes, so sorry, so long.
Long way from Story County, sold for a song.
Captain Obvious: you got a lip on you.
Captain Obvious: we end each day on earth.

Some Speech

Blue in ablutions,
she blew him, the dew
in *do your duty* and in *duel.*

What we hold in our mouths
includes the hostess,
a tray of hors d'oeuvres,

summer by way of hot air. Taut
from this to that to that to that,
I scribble silly soliloquies—*I draw the line.*

Punchlines:
My father was a lollipop manufacturer.
Buddha, you fat fuck. In punchline,

punch. In punch, the palm and fingers.
The poem, a pound puppy,
whimpering for love.

No stranger to the stationary bike,
I admit I spit at the hills,
smug in their forward motion.

In this land lit by bright vowels,
I mine the ore in boredom, and redo.
In the privilege of language,

the privy and the ledge.
Behind the deli counter,
an enormous tongue.

Face for Radio

As usual I am unusually tired.
All night my fingers double-crossed me,
tangled up in someone else's hair.
Breakfast is sand with a promise of pearls.
If I were an operation, I'd be fly-by-night
and very bloody. If I were a sow, I'd be hog-tied.
I was born under the sign of the toy breed,
the yapper, if you will—and I will—on the cusp
of bikini season. Somersaults, cartwheels.
Call me poorly executed. Call me late for dinner
and a regrettable houseguest, wet towel on the bed.
Call me go-getter, meaning going going gone.
If anyone needs me, I'll be at the arcade
across from the fire station, shooting
the teeth off the cardboard clown.
If you give me a dollar I'll take my top off
and let you see my heart.

The Kisser

As in, *in the,* of course. The body knew
the drill by now. Was *are we there yet* and then
never been so, then *so long.* Heart tied
with twine, with shorthairs, trip wires—whispered *that bind.*
Drew the short straw, scared herself apart
to spit-sweet shards and into time that counted
backwards from two lips ago. Said *done*
is done and is between me and those teeth.
Some little story about dignity.
We're there yet. Said *trussed me.* Body the white flag,
body the pulley. Hoist up and sang to beat
the heart back down again—*stick-stone, stick-stone.*

Dancing with Strangers

I'll do The Worm he said,
then dropped to the floor
where he writhed alone.

I returned home and again glowing
on the lawn—white fur, blue eyes,
collarless thought of a dog.

Shuffle and clatter as the men climbed
up the embankment in the dark,
born of trains, dropped to earth

grown and lonely, bearded, wielding
bags of cans. Still bodies of junk-fish carp
caught and discarded that choked on air

and expired reeking.
And in the locked museum
all the statues hold their breasts.

The Station

Bless the men who smell like wet wool. Bless the men who scuff the floors. Bless the men with glasses glinting too large for their eyes. Bless the men with half-eaten sandwiches in mindless strangleholds spilling shredded lettuce on the tiles. Bless the men with shaved heads, those rubbing the skull's imperfect terrain and the pocked landscape of the cheek. Bless the men with hands balled in fists hiding smiles of dirt under each nail. Bless the men with matching luggage. Bless the men with misshapen duffel bags dragged by the scruff from town to town. Bless the men going home. Bless the men pretending to go home. Bless the men with brown overcoats and gray trousers, which they call *camel* and *heather*, fluent in the language of catalogues. Bless the men who argue with other men over lotto picks. Bless the other men too. Bless the men who blow against a cup of coffee as if it were the final candle on a birthday cake, a wish aching to crescendo between their temples. Bless the men drumming their heels against the wooden benches. Also the men with comb-overs like secrets spoken. Bless them, bless them, bless them. And please bless the men with the faces of boys. And the men missing legs, leaning on air.

Remains

Mama,
he's not like
the other coroners. → *guys only lead to pain*

Took me upstairs
and showed me
his coelacanth.

Sutured the last
of the suitors at sunup.
Straddled the strata,

solved for salve.
Same river begging
to be taken back.

Prayed effigy, efficacy,
something to sign for.
Bodies? Flutter fodder.

Fit start to endgame.
Last rites, riots,
stage left in a whisper,

best left beheaded,
behest left unsung.
Secured the parameters,

opened the aperture,
cut me a switch
and learned luck

a new trick.
Wind turned tail,
broke stride and won

over, air on the side
of the nacreous acreage,
my far cry.

God Bless Our Mess

Day by day, the days dissolved into the simplest of cross-stitched requests.
The sky let herself go—a fistful of sleet, a leftover moon.

Looking down became a hobby which payed off the morning when I found
an unmarked house key and a poorly molded plastic soldier.

On the path by the train tracks, I taught myself to recognize the marks
made by a limp in snow, shuffle in snow, stagger through snow.

There were calls to field, long-distance. Also, catcalls from moving trucks.
Some days I drove by Every Bloomin' Thing and was tempted to turn off

into the parking lot and march into the greenhouse, remove my scarf and gloves
and stand bare-chested, crying *pothos, ficus* until I grew moss or was dragged away.

Some days I reached for my turn signal but kept driving. Thus, the weeks looked
like this: Monday—small claims court, Tuesday—leaky vessel,

Wednesday—scratched laugh track, Thursday—ritual burial, Friday—
blank check, Saturday—strip mall, Sunday—closed concession stand.

Another refrain snagged in my mind like a hangnail on some sweater's pilled knit—
lit from within lit from within it went as I watched other women emerge orange

into the winter night, the sky a contusion, the streets all slush and no action,
their backs to a borrowed summer, to the bright lights of Jamaica Me Tan.

My First Creation Myth

God, grant me vacancy. In the rain, all bets
are off. We take pot shots at low-hanging stars,
translate the heart's quaint tribal vernacular,
mistake *holiday* for *holocaust*, go into hiding.
He writes a poem about lilies and lo and behold,
the flower casts its thick-stalked shadow across
the gravel path. Behind the blinds, we undress
for the mirror. In the dark, a hat and coat hung
in conjunction become a lonely man.
I hug his limp body, slip chocolate
in his pocket, wear him out into the night.
You never run out of good ideas he says.

I peed in the shampoo, Spence. What now?
He says *too many cowboys spoil the cow.*

17

Goodbye, I Love You

The clown to his paramour:
Strap on your stilts and show some wooden leg.

To each, a top hat and an earful of dimes,
laughter as the laxatives kick in on the big screen.

The eyes are the windows to the sockets.
The way to a man's heart is through his ribcage.

What separates us from the air
is our skin, the loaded body's holster.

The drunk boyfriend of the mathematician:
Equate this, bitch.

How good it feels to pick the cyst
in the sunny apartment, crowing *I've been wronged.*

In the diner, promise of condiments and a sign declaring
Quiet Dinning. Outside, toilet paper blooms in the trees.

The poet gets kinky:
Turn off the light and tug my heartstrings.

What separates us from the children of the same name
is the botched prom night, the drooping boutonniere.

No crime to leave, tail between some stranger's legs.
Yes, urge to live a montage, bodies spliced inside a song.

What separates us from the apes is the radio,
each Sunday reborn to a new Top 40.

Still, no cure for the foot-in-mouth fetish:
Hey, aren't you the man who's dying?

Can't Get There from Here

On car trips, word games—
love into glove into globe, lobe, lose, lost, last.
Refusal of the helmet and the wind spins tangles
through my hair. The highway eyes my body,
lolling its black tongue.

Congratulations to the doctors
who discovered a low flat organ in the belly
whose only function is to ache upon leaving.
Follows that they then absolved the heart,
brave little engine. That the function of trains
is transport, not sadness, and the whistle's pang
is simply some dark sleight of hand.

Flight and in-flight meals, condiments, commitment—
slather mustard and muster courage for descent.
What goes up must adjust its cabin pressure.
What goes down must go down gently or burn.

*moving on from
loss / end*

Apology

Days were display dives, sure swoop.
Then sudden flutter and fall through to triage

and the queue of singe, blister, callous, soar
to sore heart sinking teeth into skin.

I beat at the skylight, threw voices
to nimbus, my lawless frontier.

I was a windpipe when I met my love,
and he, a storm surge, lightened air

and lifted water, urgent. Now, body spent,
find me unflappable, framed with his feathers,

self-evidence, see, the straw we drove
into the post as he scattered my ashes

and spun me up, a wild vane.
What's to trust a rusted trestle?

One last gust and I'll return these wings.

Physical Education

A shake required his hand in mine.
A shiver I could execute alone.
We knew heartbreak would take

a bone saw and a rubber glove.
Night brought emissions against interest.
His hand beneath the steering wheel

and up my skirt was not a moving
violation. Yes meant yes.
All emotions were small emotions,

moans finite as breath.
We were born of blood.
Foolishness to command the body

to take root and to blossom
and yet the clouds were all enthralled,
piled for a better view, watched

us lather in the outdoor shower,
then told the ocean of their findings
as they opened into rain.

Commitment

I should shut up. Crescendo
to one raised eyebrow,
stranger saying *better to end with apology*
than begin with permission.
I claim these months alone
to be Semester at Sea, *largesse*,
excessive gifting, *large ice*, a looming
at the prow. I begin the bargaining
with *drop anchor,* marry entrance to exit,
forget the proper names of trees.
So this is the thick of it.
The handlebar explodes the neon vacuum.
I can't remember history but I heard it was bad.
The stranger tries critique, calls my gun *too loaded.*
Later, party tricks. He plucks *carnation* from *incarnation.*
Butter knife, bone saw, all my questions
of tooth and scale. Who are we and why are we yelling?
Are those real ponies? Whose blood?
Flatworm implies judgment. *Butcher* implies
judgment. *Harder* implies judgment.
In the river, diagonal drift of kick and pull,
current compromising with my stroke.
Thick log pinning logic, dinner's anatomy,
chicken legs and chicken fingers.
Still, surplus of sturdy nouns—Pen. Man. Ship.
On the bridge, a burning car.
Him, port city. Me, boom town.

The record skips from *you're pretty* to *you're pretty
much welcome any time.* All my sparkly vows:
Run. Be amazing. I understand
how birds must fear the long arm
of the window washer, the clean pane.

I'm Rubber, You're Glue

In the front yard, the manic coupling of rabbits.
You've been sulking since I let slip my belief
that the bonsai is just a small tree,
dance, a weak impersonation of birds and machinery.
Isn't every dance a mating dance?
It started when you snarled
don't wear the birthday hat if it's not your birthday.
It started when I told your mother
I'm not afraid of strangers, I just don't like you.
Sometimes we mistake silence for choking,
break each other's ribs.
The elms say *settle*, the trains say *move*.
The yellow light says *good luck*,
but then turns red, muffles a laugh as we pass.

Getting Cold, Eh?

Across the street at Lensing, the first hearse of the season scudded past the pillars. I was napping in the orange porch chair, startled from the stage of a dream peopled with the old jokes' cast: the lollipop manufacturer, the rabbi, plus-size bunny, someone's momma, a passel of fair-haired ladies, dead baby, bee and wasp, two gay Irishmen, repeat offender molester, the well-endowed. The others looked on as Patrick Fitzgerald told Gerald Fitzpatrick, *the love is gone and any chimp could kiss my shoulder blades at night.* The others made suggestions: standardized testing, a dance-a-thon, enforced bird watching, shorter skirts for schoolgirls, a cake fight, a modicum of decorum, legal adoption of homunculus and incubus. Gerald claimed claustrophilia, begged the crowd to hold him tight. I surfaced as the rabbi shouted that purpose is a porpoise, click and blowhole, because it speaks does not mean that we understand. Then the mourners with Midwestern accents: *roof* like the dog's bark, *root,* a road's undoing.

Respects

Fancied herself a cobbled hobbyhorse,
baubles, glue, a wobble in the ducts.
After the last dirge, escaped to the annex,
pressed against the taller pall bearer beneath
a winding-sheet, murmured *accrete already*.
Skin's rash decisions, raised red and rubbed
him the wrong way. Woe is what, again?
No accident. Penitent. Held back a hiccup,
straddled the teeter-totter, ponied up to slip
her shirt off and proffer her bright tongue.

Consolation Prize

With morning came the urge to pull up my pants
and escape through the dog door. Sometimes I wanted
to kiss all the men and sometimes I did, not as simple
as relax and be lonely since my hands were so cold.

In the rain, the town smelled like piss and French fries.
The men grew mustaches to shave them off.
With the shades drawn, we compared
scars and birthmarks, tried on the big desires.

Later I told them I mistook head for moon and moved
closer to find the famous face. I told them my lips paid
the standing ransom, forked over the tongue.
Further down the page, the river bent at the fairgrounds

that once starred in the fictions of childhood,
a box in my closet still filled with cramped cursive
in which the clowns embraced the girls
behind the Tilt-a-Whirl. Always the urge to close

the gap between the X's and the slack-jawed O.
In spring ground, bulbs shrug and shift and whisper
time to change our lives but it was not spring then
and the bulbs hunkered in the frozen dirt

and in the wind the skin of our knuckles cracked.
With morning came a trail of single earrings, rubber bands,
spit-out gristle and split ends. I blamed tequila,
the way the men would lick and salt and lick their hands,

then pucker of lime and a swooning.
Again, again. Variations on a theme of gravity—
Wing Night every Monday, us cheering as the athletes lunged
at earth and at each other on the screens above the bar,

us sucking the tiny bones and then each finger.
Once I asked the men if they remembered
being small and how we hid behind the school
with a can of hairspray and lit its mist into a burst of fire.

Self-Portrait with Family Tree

They pull my puppet limbs to twitching
back to the horse thief and the rabbi's daughter,
the pervert and the coroner, the witch killer, the judge.

Panting from nipping the tip of my tail, I hang my pointed hat.
They were the dogs and they were the dog-eat-dogs,
and some of them died virgins and some of them died trying,

and some of them ate nothing and said they were stuffed,
and some of them ate crow all night and woke with feathers
between their molars and hollow bones beneath their beds.

If this house caught fire I'd grab my red boots
and the chess set with the chewed-up queen.
This morning I called my mother to tell her the one

about the interrupting starfish but couldn't finish
as the punch line was my open hand,
palm and all five fingers on her face.

Note to So Sorry for Self

I hope you like dirt because that's what you're getting.
Can't stop held over or ahead, bloodletting
go. En route to apeshit, look up the old address,
stand on the lawn yelling fill in my blanks. Best
left unsaid: *Oops.* Here's looking. Yup,
paper cut to the quick is to say quit moping,
my prize pumpkin, my favorite mammal.
Whole town's seen through the dress rehearsal,
best and brightest dramaturges parsing
the flamingo routine, blistered foot tucking
up into darkness. No use crying over erosion—
all soil's slipped soil. Hung over my head on
nobody's shoulders. All skin's slipped skin,
sure collision—insides out and air wants in.

Cold Weather

Now scribbled letters from the ghosts I know the best—men built from bones of contention, women from hair matted against the drain, the horny linguist who eyes the tongue, sad starlet muttering stage directions, spectral ex-girlfriends wielding their housecats, hirsute ghosts of coaches past declaring *you run until I'm tired.* I don't reply, can't raise their spirits with this silly alphabet, *A* standing splay-legged, *B* in her padded bra. Instead, gnawed pen, gooseflesh and a mad dash to the photo booth, urge to verify my face, gray litany of grins and grimaces. Meanwhile, riddles—*what is the sound of one hand pinned behind your back?*

Yes, I'm scared the dead will make their problem mine, come pop my heart, that party favor fashioned from a length of red balloon. At night I pray for growth but not growths, *that's swell* not *that's swollen,* trains every hour on the hour, no lightning but fireworks, lit fuse and a lightening sky. Alone, I whisper *encore,* whisper *anchor,* flash familiar shadow puppets at the wall, same laughing dog again, again. *Good luck,* they say, *with blood and breath and what the air scares out and what the earth beats from your body: piss, bejeezus, stuffing, tar.*

Them's Fighting Words

[handwritten: relationship is demise]

[handwritten: deck of cards; fate]

You left the party and I checked the deck, found I was missing
my suicide king—full blown and come to blows and left
full well enough alone, rose from the playing dead
to heads or cocktails, full-contact chatterboxing, standing
water and standing bets. Cry *uncle*, tweaked nipple and *whistle
or you lose it,* mechanical bullfight running on empty threats.
Now solve for *x* where mph is speed and *oomph* is impact
and the tip of the tongue sticks to tip of the iceberg
and now the slow part where the whole plot's read out loud—
and in the next panel, the big gun says pkow pkow pkow.

[handwritten: arguments]

[handwritten: relates back to suicide king]

Ante

full throttle to choked forward motions denied saw her tailspin and raised her
a nosedive all pressing questions applied to the wound saw the romeo saw the
tango jilted the juliet quick as a foxtrot spin around the blocked advance meant
tip off bet on that glass bedroom eye and near miss sighted saw her cherry and
raised her on top of a lucky breaking point game point and stare and played her
where she lay and lied about her whereabouts and said great mindless always
think a likely story raise their hackles and rise to the bait the grin saw bared it all
indentured gift horse raised a sprint some spirit fingers hunted marching pecked
for orders cried dear diarist sinking shipmate still my best man overboard to
raise a bucket saying need an extra hand to bail the blood now look what a
mess you've made of that heart

Sound Bites

This week, cheap Valentines.
Sign says half price, bee says Bee Mine.
At home, the sheets say a little blood
goes a long way. The list says dog food
and onions. The neighbor's lazy gun says
what'll they do, fire me? Hand says
clap and the trees throw crows.
Whatever the sky says is old news.
Rented house: don't leave me like this.
The dog begins to pant and piss:
I never said I was your friend.
Summer: Strip. Winter: The End.
Before you say anything babe, I should say
ix-nay on the es-yes-yay, on the ove-lay.

Trick or Treat

Mom stood out front, negotiating with the falling leaves. Dad cheered her on, yelled *tough love* from the upstairs window. The small kids had to be home by dark and so, late afternoon, the green-faced and the bloody and the crowned all drifted up the walk. In the locker room, the boys undressed and compared the size of their sadness while the girls, mid-epidemic, could say nothing but *I dare you*. I was spared, somehow. I kicked up dust and whispered *eat my dust*. I saw the crows eyeing the dog and whispered nothing. I overheard Dad say to Mom one night *the sky has got the upper hand*. They said I was a good egg. They said if I chose to draw the house, I should add shingles with a felt tip pen. That year, I wore a hat, added a mustache to my upper lip with eyeliner, jutted my hips and called myself *cowboy*. I loved a robot who ate even the unwrapped candy. When I returned home, the television murmured of cut funding, of the satellites struck dumb and blind, careening through what we called outer space.

Pocket Money

"presents" do not seem all sweet

For sweet sixteen, a box of monoxide,
a letterpress broadside, a spaniel, a brooch.
Not your grandmother's old scepter,
rather, petty cash under petticoats,
teeth eclipsed in a mouthful of crowns.
They let the little half-wit build a birdhouse,
try her hand at the circular saw.
Stuffed her face with powdered donettes.
Slept on the ottoman sopping wet.
Delicate dear melted salver to silver,
bothered her pretty little head.
Later exchanged the Geiger counter
for a cue and cue ball, racked, broke.

Lying Down with ~~Dogs~~ men

Fetch this phenomenominal conjesture. This time I mean it. A wag of the wand and the restive history sits like a sure thing. Suppositious (delicious) hypotheosis. Like lips could love a rubber teat. Miss *stay*, miss *beg*. Mistake the clock's tick-tock for some synecdochetic-tocking heart. No such touch as specious scratch of scruff or tummy. Name the litter after our best senses—Salty, Sweet, Sour, True and False. Lexiconic misprojections, *good* is *good* for ours and only, subspurious as in—if that's a puggle, my Grandpa's a cockapoo. Grandma's a labradoodle. Belly up's uncle and auntie's asleep at the top of the weaning pile. Paws is a cheap shot. Make it feel real like aposiopesis like—but never mind. This is *what army* sanitized for your protection. Mine match the alleles on the leash in question. Curled with the girls like a six-pack of commas. Got my licks in. Got my chihuzzahs. Sure I'm guilty. My dream date's to dig to China. Tongue to every spill and tail between. Haven't heard the last of Grandma. Ask any canny canine if it's rough. It's rough. I do it every chance I get.

Heaven

Please be my date
to this evening's disaster.

A bit lip. The tip
of the tip off, you,

beginning
of my ever endless.

Apples fallen
on the launch pad.

Sun racing down
without a parachute again.

In event of horizon,
lie low and alone.

Underpass and overpass
crisscross the fault.

Raze the last
of the orchard.

Raise the blackened banner.
Lower your right hand.

Quick Study

Put a hold on the have and to hold'em's a game,
bets half-cocked at the big dogs, one shoe
on and running, chicken's a nickname
and nick's just a cut. Let me get you

where you want me, paint on some tight pants
and varnish the town. Call means I've got
your number. Fold means no chance,
each night cut from the same bolt

of cloth. Never say never mind,
never turn your back to back or show
your hand in mine. What's mine
is minor but it still feels good to know

you and I could be big blind and small blind,
Adam and odds and even Eden this time.

Where Babies Come From

She ditched the dignitaries at the arboretum,
puttyroot in a gunnysack, big bulb and all.
Shoulder to grow light, ducked

to where water was foam, final.
Slipped into something a little more shiftless.
Talked archaeopteryx. Slammed a mimosa.

Fingered malignant, then rigged
a slingshot at the quay, waggled sayonara
to spinster spitting cuticles into the bassinet,

spinster smuggling cigars in her girdle,
spinster who bled from her mustache on Sundays,
spinster who fondled the farsighted carhop,

ruined the solitaire deck in the sauna.
Sun dappled a brindled dog. Lifted hackles,
then back to licking its nethers and chops.

On a hunch she checked the lost-and-found,
dug up her first school frock and an eyelet punch.
Broke the flange, promised a lariat, saw a man

about his mother. Butts in the jack-o-lantern,
ash on the hassock. *Arrivederci? You dare me?*
Asked her back Thursday to scare him some more.

Joyride

In lieu of a shoulder it's moon and a guard rail
sky as per starstruck an autograph seeker
an ambulance chaser slow slide past the on-ramp
no traffic no shoulder a dark wood the river
some invitation each dim constellation
[drunk river to moon *say "I lied and I'm sorry"*
moon to the river *I can't give you Mars.*]
A dark wood a river shot stars falling dumbstruck
the road a stiff drink and the off-ramp a chaser
the on-ramp an in-joke *forget that I said that*
some consolation each dim constellation
and as per the guard rail the road's a straight shooter
[the river's a letter *regret to inform you*
moon plays the dummy *you've got the wrong gal.*]
The sky a blank cue card the road claiming asphalt
a dim abdication rail begs for collision
the river prays *risen* spits at the moon and says
[*slip and fall down here—I'll hold your face under
until you quit laughing and cough up that light.*]

Small Ending

Each bird a yard bird
and wind throwing weight,
I know where you live,

wind wanting in
and the same *smack dab,*
the *best served chilled,*

bones aspiring
to *bone dry,* the last light
casing the empty house,

fist and fistula,
flesh a fixed fight,
the blind turn, the drive-thru

and the *bless you,*
apt signage (Yield),
and days and still no sign

of sky, aspiring scarecrows
(our outstretched arms)
and the days, moving targets,

trains mourning their own
and open-mouthed meters
and *I reckon* and we reckon.

Relatively Long Arms

For his sake I steered clear of *flicker,*
singed the noodles, sang for supper—
sundown at last on the bad-news New Year—
hung left, left and cut to quicker,
steered clear of *neon* but stoked the fire
with a store-bought log. Flame took the ticket,
twitched and admitted one—nervous romantic's
hopeless tic—*one on one,*
on one condition. Lover stuttered.
Wax log sputtered. Steered clear of *taxi*
but brought him a present, unwrapped the itch
I made from scratch. *Longing's been*
a long time coming. Ask me if
we're nowhere yet. Earth? Old girl got
the spins, closed her eyes and rubbed
for stars, twirled to new resolutions,
a circular saw-to, saw him a round peg,
me, square hole made do. Clear of *crosswalk.*
Oh to try a tighter orbit,
snag the scarf in the celestial machinery,
pull him so close he can't tell
his bell from my whistle, tell him
tell the moon that Dora sent you.

Director's Cut

Opening shot: morning. Mid-May. Mid-maybe,
misgiving, mistake, mid-take your time repeating after me
so long, so longing, lost and short of breath. Start
to finished lines means each between-the-line by heart

where hem reacts to haw—close shot—the big to-do list,
lights and stunts, month and mouth made-up to fit
the ending. Try the goodbye on for size. Lather, rinse, *→ shower reference*
repeat sweet nothings, catch phrase and a slow release.

The shower scene fades to soliloquy, last forwarding address
on the saloon soundstage, fired blanks, ketchup on a blouse, *→ infertility*
then aftermath and ever after. I have to say,
the camera loves you when the credits roll and you play

dead. Fast forward and you flail out like my marionette.
Rewind, you ride right backward toward me out of that sunset.

Oh My Obit

Born to a flock of odd ducks and covers,
she claimed tremor and more, stop, dropped
and rolled over. Then last wave and a wink
from her (not a dry) eye, *goodbye good alibi*
to a banner crop of hems and haws, to the cat
and the tongue, the yay and naysayers, to the one
in the win column, to the sheets to the wind.
Closed chapter, bent page on the same
razzle dazzle and the old off-key tune.
At dawn she struck set, took down the moon.

Pop Quiz

Twist of lime or twisted arm? Lent hand or footsie?
All the crossword puzzle nouns can't help me now—
the castle and the thistle, the roan, the vireo and jib.
Hello pursed door-to-door lip service, high horse sense.
The townsfolk squawk foxy, wave the big flag
as I offer my treaty, treatise titled Heart as Blank Check.
If tit, then tat. File under: beeswax, none of your.
Organ dolor means I'd release this sad skin.
Tactile error means wrong cheek to cheek.
I'm wetting my unicorn suit. Can't blame this mess
on the longwinded weather, cyst or whiskey dick.
Throat closed for repairs, I gag a bit, allergic
to the peanut gallery: *It's your fucking heart, man.*
I pledge a lesion, draw a spine in the sand.

Open Letter

Again I broke
eggs into breakfast, forked
eros from *huevos rancheros*,
split the silence with a sigh.

Each daydream, couplets
and coupling. You?

I'll hold my tongue
about your humdrum
muses, Pain in the Ass
and Plain Vanilla, mincing
hot and cold. Let me

justify my lament, admit
that I covet the size
of your sky.

I'm tired of wasting
my best lies on strangers.

Believe me
when I tell you I'm kept
awake by the light
from my body, splayed star.

A man

walks out of November into the moist air of the greenhouse and sits beneath the hanging ferns on the concrete floor with its dead leaves and drains and whispers *heal me*. Never hurts to ask. Yesterday he stationed himself in front of the television with a camera and captured snapshots of the women shilling mops. Then walked to town and laid his palms to the sticky linoleum of the pancake house. Ran down past the factory and out to where the land flattens, bullied by a big sky. Saw a fallen bicycle that did not move to greet him and a dead raccoon that did not move to greet him and a rusted trestle that did not move to greet him and the brown river that moves slow over lost tires but not to greet him. This is where I could tell you *he ascends to heaven among the begonias* but that's just not possible.

Speech! Speech!

What luck even a happy beginning
If anyone asks we can say we were praying
Sea legs ready steady rudder
First foray to impossibly softer

Apple of my apogee
Landlocked island's delicacy
Sunday punch boxful of squashes
Buttercup Carnival Delicata

Spell called for chrism and husks of cicada
For pinch the pods from Mama's catalpa
And scrap the stratagems one two three
Admit without question the question begged me

Here's my dear a redder riddle
Heads and legs but where's the middle
Where'd you find time to dry your eyes
Christen our little alibi

Scratch sunset clause and finder's fee
I want you watching when the sun slips into me

Forever Hold Your Peace, Speak Now Or

Fancied myself
a fine receptacle

for as they say
discarded sharps

and you my
miracle-cum-miracle

in deaf gone blind
water to wind.

How did we aim
to figure or to ground?

Here lies the dowry hid
beneath my tongue.

Ours a most venial
vernacular—do I make

you happy did I
make you happy?

Fiddler's Money

Thimblerigged with baby's milk teeth.
Sleight-of-hand and switched to swindle.
Stuffed ballot-box with finger cymbals.
Quite a clatter morning after.
Stuck out a tongue and it froze to the fulcrum.
Now, sotto voce: *Holy flagellum.*
Cut the baloney. You and what army?
Don't fret, hollow body, broke in the flail.

The End

Then they faced each other
on the porch and divvied up
the insults. He kept fussbudget,
bawl-baby and swivel-headed nabob.
She kept jerk, cock, pansy, clown.
Goodbye to the games of day-to-day,

she said, Peekaboo and Doorbell Ditch
which ended in splayed fingers
and an empty stoop as they vied
for the giving end of each disappearing act.
If she closed her eyes, he couldn't see her.
She closes her eyes and he can't see her

bearing down now on this distance and barreling
past the sod farms in the pig-smelling air,
listening to the faulty heat shield,
which sounds to her like a man beating
a robot with a spoon, clattered complaints
from the car's most dark and private parts.

Break, Make Or

Unseemly to dream in green each night sleep
through the entire moon lids on or else an eye
boils over. Rattle the sabers through void
of course and claim a brighter phase. Teetering
on a flimsy peduncle all petal and heavy head
and nothing afield that the mower would stop for.
Aspire to symbolic shovelful forever mourn
the severance of the lesser hissing heads.
Binoculars backwards closest call to distance
as in redwing flipped to a fleck on a lens.

My Kingdom for the Pretty Picture

Gave all the good ears for a warmer whisper.
Skinned the same day and so kept forever.
Slipped stitches known to keep each other's secrets.
Each forked stick stripped and strung to shoot.
A sliver of mirror's still an honest mnemonic.
Some assembly required for martyr of choice.
The hard hats disappeared somewhere in transit.
Gait of split knees and pressed palms into lists.
Save plinth and parapet the town was mist,
missing. Shook in the face of the sun's red fist.

Score

Beneath the girder, fingers,
five finer points dipped to a bowl
of lemon water, lifted dripping.
Larvae feeding on the onions.
Bone ash in the porcelain.
Slept through the sonata, seasoned
to taste and simmered, lashed
the laths and dropped anchor.
Beneath the curtsy, a batch
of gingersnaps were priced to burn.

Flight, Fight Or

Every rearview a lovescape of ex-towns.
Bumper to bumper dear what do you heart?
I favor my left side I favor leaving.
My pheasants can fly but they'd rather run.
Never said feather oars or father me.
Where recipe calls for apricots try fog.
There should have been a strap from yoke to harness.
For record whatever I never kissed the bride.
Here lies the sigh begun nine lines ago.
I miss your wingspan miss your hollow bones.

Our Fair Sentence

Those days were still wearing their brand-new welcomes,
putting one word—world—in front of another, blazonry
and all good faith therein where was writ dexter, sinister,
pick a number. Any everyman was proud to proclaim
the state of *even our disaster's faster*, trophies soldered
fist to plinth to tower over in precipitous dazzle down
to the waterlogged potter's field in which listed fits pitched
for the night, the beaten band and the broken bank, the seep
where the earth wept up its ichor, war cry whittled to dumb
ditty—*shoot first, shoot later*—dialectic left for dead and
the closest exit indeed behind us by way of frayed refrain:
say *when,* say when.

Copy That

Please refrain touch to our foregones.
They's brains' ballast one conditions.

Pre-dark days of harsh geometry
we could call *all* those shapes diamonds.

Wheeled in what a whiny gurney.
Spun us some such glib and slippery.

Now lookie here it's poor man's Twister
bare boards to our trip and tangle

right foot blue and right red handed
joie de veuve win lose malinger.

Took home a prize for best-dressed marauder.
A drag of that river. Some silly trick

to balance on hindsight. Don't give us that
it's sunrise somewhere. Try a prayer:

Almighty please bother to jiggle the handle.
Please press us at least a wine of the pickings.

This machine steam cleans.
This machine ends presidents.

Who's you to finger? Rather be raining.
Maybe it's just my amygdala talking.

Manifest presto. Some greener dollar.
Maybe tomorrow's marrow matches.

What I wouldn't give for a well-trained angel
with a whole damn trigger hand.

Hush Money

Pretend this is legal. Pretend this is tender.
Composed of one carpel a pistil is simple.
Inside the engine, the piston's a-thrusting.
Spleen's an impostor, gland-like but ductless.
Chrysanthemums bloom and God's in Havana.
Shift the sandals and stand agape.
The corpse is in the copse, of course.

Go, Touch And

Splint? Hot glue? How to un-break
the news that no one's better yet.
Ho-hum undone sword to end all
shoulders leaner now alee and in lieu
of, after a fiercer math of red subtractions.
Last one rites is a rotten tug of warning.
What nerve we had to press the pontiff,
wear the pants in any pantheon. Here
lies here lies. File under human interest.
File under fluid in the lungs.

Hearth and Home

And baby made jar-bound, netted himself
a calico pennant, spangled skimmer to beat
and blunder under glass. Silent raffle
in the old gymnasium, bit lip, watched
mama lick nib, scrawl bids and win
the Chinese mustard fine print swore
the only condiment you'll ever need.
This foyer is no wind-swept lake.
Gave baby the spoils to feed to the drain.
Sun on parquet. Shards took to task. Tipped
dustpan to dustbin, shook the ripped wings.

A Light Touch

The dinner guests weren't looking
when the wet nurse led him upstairs
to the linen closet and unfastened,
slipped a Save the Date card
between his waistband and the scar.
Smell of the elm's inner bark
and an aftertaste of zinc and copper.
Did baby miss his canapés?
Below, a wink and sudden tidbit,
a swallow lodged inside a throat.

Thread the Needle

Stitched her up pretty as anything again.
By noon, joined hands with the row of girls.
Ran under their arms, still holding
her neighbor. Fair game until the bag
of blood and catgut fell. Was whist.
That night, burdened, dreamed baling hay.
Woke swaddled, sweating, wrapped
in the big loom's length of lace.
In this case, by machines, for machines.
From the start, the eye was at the pointed end.

The Little Hours

She opened the east egress, breezed up.
He held the horse's hoof to trim
scarred skin from fetter bone.
Dog-eared diurnal lost in the pasture.
Primer laid down on three of four walls,
dropped the brush to splay in clover
and cover his eyes. Past bearded iris
and beardless iris, black-and-blue
damselfly fell to a swallow where before
was body dragged dead from the head
of water meant to turn the wheel.

Big Money

Lady of the Laundromat says toss the shirt
or dip the other sleeve in blood.
Coquette thinks *cockatrice,* runs to the matinee
to miss the eclipse. For old time's sake,
she throws on her ape mask.
Already funding for dragging the river.
She thinks she'll take *that body* when she goes.

Flora and Fauna

He watched me witness my own hands
whorled wrung and open to flutter unfurled.
Hushed hearsay passed finger to finger,
harbored heresy, palm foretold
a *live forever then walk home,*
a scream-strung sun streaming *worship me.*
Mess of snapdragons and scurf, day-lilies
come hell-bent, bouquet of *have my way with*
tied with twine and piano wire
tuned to *take that tone.* In the blind

I meant *don't take* and flushed—fashioned
a thicket from twigs and hot glue, played pleaser,
came seamless, cooed *like what I see through you.*
Came to his feeder and held my wings
until, tired of purpling for the cause,
the awe-worn knees swore off swooning,
unbent me to standing, told me of a bough
by the river bent to water. If he asks after me,
I'm now full and grown green—whisper
can't miss me, body of blossoms, this yield.

Cube of ice my incubus slid a-nape

and downy upside over crown's a proper
interregnum, even some for later
under nail. Keened my pieces, the darling
ineffer, in pidgin and furious Braille,
backbone gone glockenspiel, glister to gliss
to pass on the narrow, mallet to marrow's
carillon, aspiring, borrowed a bigger hammer
and two jaws, a shiv, a shim to slip a-level,
a lever to makeshift a sleep-on-it grip. I wore
my smoke ring and best end-of-days face,
saw sunrise and thought *looks expensive*, hoarded
my morphemes, monads, minims, not a spare
pixel for system malfunction, plume in a flap,
mote in a pother, pottle of anything other
than fix-it and on-your-way. Hours of most
of me held above my heart, wind in my
everything and waited. Wondered my weight
in *what for*, engendered. Asked ever-after'd
still grit for the signet, press each petal
brittle, breathe to shallow bits the deep
beneath what I was up against.

Flight

A dream I woke once
to write down and again
to discard. More than
the hopeful mouthful,
quick blood in my own
hands held, wings set.
Familiar feathers on
an updraft in air, akin
to swimming. Sure,
and the wires swap
sparks to defend
high heaven, voices
sublime into alchemic
voltage. Void between
stars and the word *stars*
rattles, black saber.
Even in air I'm foolish
and too full to float.
I want my feet to fire
where fire spews
boosters, where
boosters lash to orbit,
where I can call a star
a star and ball my blood
when my blood slips.
Forget the flap or wait
for wind. I want inside
ballistic body, pressed

to trajectory, prescient
trajectory, mouth in
my throat as if this fast
or *nothing*, which is not
the same as space.

Canzone: How To

Fetch was the double gave and took to where the eye formed
I, weighed its sameness. Mirror leered and signed the line
like one's done was one's doing. Cramped hand, pro forma.
A marked man in a marksman's glass. *Regret to inform*
mouthed mine to signet. Doubled over. Saint prayed
for a burden and received the cruciform
cartilage knot in her heart, cuneiform
deformation folded in to find at the end.
I call love letter. What say you, gristle? Bend
and spell *what's mine is mine*. Word my mark. Form
thorn or bloom but plait to plead my case with just one
blessing, a hook in my heart to hang a hat on.

Bless pried the dead lips open. *Wound* on tongue one
and *bow* on tongue two tied to *blood* and *knee* where form
and function fused as vessels to even the hardest bone
remember. I hinged and dripped as good as anyone,
dug heels and claimed keeper, refused to loose the tumpline
on an incline or ever, wore *you shall bind* hard-won,
form-fitting. How then hold in mind the bloom in this one's
hand was thorn in that one? Hoist the hyssop spray
to turn lintel to slashed vein, split lips open in prayer.
Past tense is too easy, turns tale vestigial only,
an ensign colored quarantine unfurling endless
whether or not I admit to belief in an *endless*

at all. Exeunt every other other. Try this end—
aposteme, apostrophe, purulent, alone.

By and for hands bound as verso, recto, bookends
and naught beyond the page. File as full bleed. Send
proofs, proof. Spine same as any fold. Need not form
a scab as strikethrough fixes a less sticky mend.
Sure saddle-stitched and prone to creep. Gutter bends
backward, part undisciplined disciple sidelined
past perfect, part participle—*written, unwritten*—lines
run-on or fragment, never not dangling at the end.
But no. I'd rather atoms, stomata, pores, ropes and pray
it's ever in me, trinket in the kingcake, my prize.

Suck the joke clean of apocryphal marrow. Pry
the tin tiara off, ring a rash and so ends
jester sinister and jester dexter. Fall prey
to the tune of *what say you* and not a prayer
between the two. I still want to *be* one, *the* one,
catch my? Prostrate yes but fell flat. Mine mien, prithee—
who's heard means to a beginning? No proper prayer,
this sprinter's crouch, slide and slip-thrust, profane form.
Think bigger. Take the suit out, find fit to be formed
to a wider load. Here wouldn't hurt to praise
the hills, horizon's good measure and the fault line
where what's under rubs for friction, counts timeline

and fracture its due and fire its bottom line,
aspires back to sand and always hungry. Preys
on its own edges as on every other line.
Maxilla, mandible, wants to line
its maw with more maw. Open wide's again the end
of every shudder. *Come closer* or you'll miss your lines
and no prompter. I know this trick. Above the skyline,
even my flying dreams are flailing dreams, one

heaven-rapt wing gives the stars a run for, one
defrocked and fit only to fall. Above the tree line,
places, places coaxes constellations into uniform,
connects *ta-da* dots post-stutter—*ta-ta ta-ta*—to form

keel, keyhole, crux. Ember clutter. Come on, perform.
What say you, still small voice? Static's elision, eleison,
calm in the beholder's eye, means to mend, amend.
I'll wait. No stranger's tongue whereon the prayer
worth its amen needs eons just to say *align*.

Spectrum

Try a red wafer on white paper.
By holding, made whole, holy,
so sepulchered. Above, surplus
of sepals, borne bracts, a garden
throwing up her hands, spectacle,
green specter, then gone. Brace
your capillaries, babe. Today's
family is a mouthful: moth, farther,
bother, cistern. Look. There's
the orphan's orphan boarding a bus.

Body Language

I know the route by heart means this town winds inside me—the street of low trees. The street of bad smells. The street of jostling. The street of downcast eyes. The street of phantom cries and phantom bells. Still, the heart, a glove compartment crammed with flares and old maps. What I thought was a brief goodbye folded in thirds on the kitchen table was last month's electric bill. Filament, firmament, old classics of earth and light. The horizon is a given, and the last light holding the horizon, and the lit billboard selling smiles, the gin and nosy girls and noisy boys, the highway's shoulders smeared with the head wounds of dropped deer, the yellow beetles and their fecal smell of earth, each bank vying for the river's lick and whisper. Our inheritance—flags limp in a windless October, all our parents' cancers, the dog gnawing his blighted tail. Always the conversation turns to lack of rain, to withered corn, beef's fallen status among the meats. This is no country of columns and cologne, rather, red welts, welding, hardy composites of steel and mules. Heat rash. Razor burn. Birth, an excuse for birthmarks. The body coughing, slouching, sloughing. Isn't all flesh proud flesh? Having studied history, the initial response is to dance around the question. Having spent the last dollar on the jukebox, the initial response is to dance.

Yes, I cross my legs and bolt my door, read *boys/girls* as *boys slash girls*. The dog pants over panties, I leave lollipops on the graves of my favorite dirty men, pray and play favorites—Our Lady of Kept Secrets, Patron Saint of the First Frost. At night, the bars blaze neon, the streets lit like the lost need finding. He says *attention*, I hear *a tension*. At last call, charades, miming *I can't do this*, miming *yes yes yes*. Yes, I'm still proofreading my body, adding punctuation, long ellipses between kisses. Back on the bicycle, I coast past the scaffolding, the orange cones, the rolls of insulation. Here, construction's no construction—real dirt. Afternoons, the children study anatomy, repeat *lumbar, femur, stirrup, supine.*

When they say *our cells turn over,* they mean they're gone. Flip the mattress, beat the rug. Carouse between laundry days, then wander from machine to line with pants in hand.

The lines blur between my nouns and verbs. *Summer. Fist.* Failed ad campaigns—*cut out the middleman, break your own heart.* Then, *Nobody. No body. No, buddy.* When I say *I've got something on you,* I mean my open palm.

In town, the elderly stall traffic with their cataracts, their Cadillacs. They shake like lapless lapdogs, hear *terminal* and can't imagine the airport, bodies borne into sky. Winter won't take no for an answer. In the supermarket, speakers crooning *caught between the moon and New York City,* crying *now it's gone, gone, gone.* The women stand with their hands beneath the misting mechanisms above the tiered greens. In the basements, the spiders spin webs, the girls spin the bottle. In the morning, *see you never.* The girls sprint themselves skinny, sweat off the smell of strangers' hands. In dreams, the crawlspace, the bank queue, the stairwell, always one foot in the heart's open door. In dreams, daughters of the daughters of the Midwest, daughters stranded inland in these states of snow, daughters so pale the sun shines through their skin. Easy bird call: *sweet-sweet.* Advice: don't smoke in the silo. Whisper *wanderlust,* he'll eat out of your hand.

I do not dare ask for fruition, rather, pray for fruit, simple apple in the palm. All the would-be lawyers' delusions of prosecution, all the meat asking wood *why must we be consumed?* Yes, Death or a hawk must have a crush on me. I rise to re-gifting—blood and chunks of field mice laid along my path. God, grant me small change. Grant this flesh imminent return. When I say *make out like bandits* I mean *the end* but not The End. I mean *the end* but empty-handed, *the end* but take no prisoners, *the end* but kiss furiously under the black mask of the sky.

Dora Malech is the author of the poetry collection *Shore Ordered Ocean* (Waywiser, 2009). Her poems have appeared in *Best New Poets, The New Yorker, Poetry, Poetry London,* and elsewhere. Her work has recently been honored with a Ruth Lilly Poetry Fellowship from the Poetry Foundation, a Glenn Schaeffer Fellowship, and a residency at the Civitella Ranieri Center in Umbertide, Italy. She holds a BA in Fine Arts from Yale University and an MFA in Poetry from the University of Iowa Writers' Workshop. Malech has taught writing at The University of Iowa, Saint Mary's College of California, Victoria University's Institute of Modern Letters in New Zealand, and Augustana College in Rock Island, Illinois. She lives in Iowa City.